The Dissent

Greatness among Us

ISAIAH J. WHITE

Word Art Publishing
9350 Wilshire Blvd
Suite 203, Beverly Hills, CA 90212
www.wordartpublishing.com
Phone: 1 (888) 614 - 1370

© 2021 Isaiah J. White. All rights reserved.

No part of this book may be reproduced, stored in a retrieval system, or transmitted by any means without the written permission of the author.

Published by Word Art Publishing

ISBN: Paperback 978-1-955070-09-6
       Hardback   978-1-955070-10-2
       Ebook   978-1-955070-11-9

Because of the dynamic nature of the Internet, any web addresses or links contained in this book may have changed since publication and may no longer be valid. The opinions expressed in this manuscript are solely the opinions of the author and do not represent the opinions or thoughts of the publisher and the publisher hereby disclaims any responsibility for them. The author has represented and warranted full ownership and/or legal right to publish all the materials in this book.

Contents

Preface 1
   poem: If I Could Write 3

Introduction 7
   poem: Sincerity 9
   My Path to God 15

Near the Roots 17
   poem: Misery 19

Distinguish the Difference 25
   story: Tale of Three Warriors 27

Empirical Isn't Imperial 33
   poem: Discovery 35

Grow, Expand, Improve 39
   poem: The Sword 41

Perception 47
   poem: The Best View 49

The Plan 55
   poem: Don't Forget Me 57

You and I 63
   poem: Like Me 65

Focal Point 71
   poem: This We Will Defend 73

Recycle 79
   poem: It Won't Stop Until 81

Preface

If I Could Write

If I could write, I'd preach to the masses.
The words given to me would fill the hunger of the world.
No more starving; minds and souls are all fed.
Eradicate emptiness, because voids are filled in.
Then there would be no want or desires to steal.
Whether you read or hear, you have your next meal.
We'd all come together, with no worry of tomorrow.
Peaceful, as sheep grazing in a field,
Because our souls have heard
That we are protected, and life lies in His word.
If I could write, this is what I would do.
But since I can't, I'll just show you.

If I could write, there'd be no parched souls.
No one deserted in the desert, looking for hope.
I'd open my mind and pour out rain.
Fill dusted pockets with puddles of knowledge, not change,
Except the one they will make with the tide.
Regardless of the moon, no lows, just highs.
Liberated because their souls are hydrated.
No drop wasted, being so pure in its tasting;
I brought it from the top of a mountain.
A lot of climbing because it's from Life's fountain.
If I could write, this is what I would do,
But since I can't, I'll just show you.

If I could write, no love would go undone.
We'd all have somebody; there'd be no single ones.
At least two hits to every made album.
Everyone would have a feature; there'd no solos sung.
There would be performances of perfect duets,
And they would sing in perfect harmony.
And no matter what distractions may try to fraction,
There will be no faction in missed keys,
Because He has the master for every door.
Though your heart is sore,
through every opening you'll soar.
If I could write, this is what I would do,
But since I can't, I'll just show you.

He did write; in the beginning it was Him.
He didn't use paper and didn't use a pen.
He spoke *exist* into existence,
Brought to life past, present, and future tense.
Those that freestyle believe that they've created,
But before you put it out, He's already made it.
Lives outside of time; Genesis He invented.
We couldn't star trek if the path wasn't indented.
Writers usually pretend as we form paragraphs.
His words are for war, not props for an act.
He can write; it's a piece of who He is.
Even gave us His Word, His Son, just to show us how to live.

    This is for all. We must focus on gaining more insight to who we are as individuals. I didn't write this in favor of any system or group. I surely didn't write this to be judgmental or condescending. I wrote this because we are more than what is seen. The Proof is what you're thinking and feeling at this moment, at any given moment. These are thoughts and emotions no one will probably ever know you experience as they may venture through the same. Everyone owns these types of secrets for, we are all human. Some things we feel are fit to tell another; other words, thoughts, and emotions we keep for whatever reason.

    These untold articles report that we truly are more than what is touched, pleased, and manipulated physically. There's a portion of us that exists that cannot be seen directly, but it can be spoken to. This piece of self can be influenced, shaped, and even controlled. The scripts you read, the lyrics you hear, and the films you watch may impact this part of you if you allow them to do so. As you dive into materials created by another, remember your imperfections may be similar to theirs. Put no fault beyond their thoughts and biases.

    As you read, you will see that we all have good intentions from our points of view, but the best of intentions will not always make for good decisions. Practice caution when submerging yourself in the arts and works; they may be the floatation you need to stay above, or they may be the very weight you must let go before you sink. So I ask, What do you allow to control you? What things will you allow to control that fraction of you? As you try to draw connections between what you read and your day-to-day experience, read the pieces of work that are inserted in the beginning of the chapters to get a different perspective of what is being said.

This book is a written account of my time meditating about the things that I have read and witnessed through the scope of my faith in Jesus Christ. I aim to encourage an open mind and heart for every reader to provoke a new outlook in life. This book will not align with any one outlook. This is my exploration of Truth, traversing through the waters of "what it seems".

Introduction

Sincerity

This is my story, and I have to open with you.
I've tried to live a slow life, but wind keeps my pages flipping.
Some words are hard to understand, like hieroglyphics,
And harder to retain after you've struggled to get it.

You have your own story, yet we're on the same page.
You write your own book, but it's read the same way.
Because there reigns and resides only one Judgment,
For everything under the sun that has been published.

Yes, I've had pages ripped and lived from it,
And some have been torn out because others steal from me.
But I can't keep my cover closed, so that you can see
I'll remain revealed and expose all of my sheets.

And as I sleep, I wish that I'd written a fairytale.
Maybe something science fiction because then that book would sell.
We don't like reading about things that are real;
We'd rather stick with tabloids and magazines of the world.

Cosmo for the girls, *GQ* for the guys.
Setting goals for those images, but the pictures are lies.
A life that doesn't exist off of the page,
Because glamour doesn't exist out of a frame.

Though this may not be a bestseller,
It is guaranteed to reach the depths far beyond a cellar.
Something that will make the dark brighter than stellar
And will make you feel fresh, if you felt you're staler than
A Bible that has been left on the dresser and

Hasn't been touched in years, so the dust just settled in.
The answers to those questions we've never come to know,
But when you read this book, your eyes will never want to close
A work that's always shown but rarely seen.

Probably because we focus on the drama in our scenes
And miss reading between the lines because of lies on the screen.
Refusing to read a book, waiting until it's shown on screen;
A man had to act it for most to go and see.
And make it more dramatic for them to believe.

While others still write compositions,
While living in their convictions,
So we can read their words given as they live it.
The words given aren't supposed to save lives.
Enlightenment from God Himself just to shed light.

On the Word that is read in the dark
That came from the Blood that was bled while in our sins, we were lost.
Now being illuminated; no need for any more to be wasted
Because The Sacrifice was made, and we are found in The Word's graces.
Basking in The Light that red is a better color
Because that ink creates life, rebuilding the destruction.

What I give in this book is what has been given to me. These words have come from many sources—my faith, my loved ones, my enemies, and so on. I was raised in Southern Baptist churches, probably because my parents were. I'll claim that my parents are serious in their relationships with Christ. Their devotion is strong; their beliefs are deeply rooted. So there were rarely any days we didn't attend church. Though I had all those years of Sunday school and was baptized in the summer of 1995, I didn't understand His limitless scope and how unorthodox He could be until I got older—more specifically, until my sophomore year of high school. Before we get too far, I want to ask you, How can we understand Him more if we don't try to grasp what has already been placed in front of us?

I was in the eighth grade when my father neared the end of his career. We moved back to the part of Texas in which my parents spent a majority of their lives. During that time, I definitely lost a portion of my identity. All of what my parents had taught me—what makes a leader, being true to who I am and what we are, and to fight to keep myself distinguished—was on the verge of being completely pushed out. It wasn't about what I was doing as much as it was about the reasons I would carry through my bad ideas. I wanted to please the people I was around to be cool and fit in. Though this seems innocent (we all want to be accepted by someone) and I was never caught doing anything major, we know a person can't be simultaneously devoted to two masters. I'm grateful that people in my life at that time cared for who I truly was and not for what I was aiming to be. I started having glimpses of Real Life shown to me, when I gave my full attention to what our eyes can only see and what our minds can naturally fathom. My days have not come without some type of challenge since then.

My change in high school started with a series of visions about tornadoes, which I felt at the time were chasing me. In the last episode, I finally gave in. It was then that I understood that it was a call for me to go higher and change my current state of mind. Those fragments were soon followed by other dreams that turned out to be metaphors of what I was soon to experience in life, specifically relationships that were going to be tested and why they would be tested. On the nights that I didn't have anything so vividly shown to me, I would wake up with an abundance of energy between 3:14 and 3:23 a.m. and feel a need to open my Bible. It was like having a craving or addiction. That experience is not strange to believers of Christianity, but it is strange to someone who has never been so close to any type of Spiritual Favor. What was also uncommon about these ordeals was that after reading the passage, however long it was, I would be overwhelmed with exhaustion as if I were rudely awakened. Later, I realized that I should incorporate those readings into my day, so I started writing them down along with their respective dates.

As I oriented myself in relation to The Map, I was warned of the hardships to come along the journey. People who attend church, temple, synagogue, Mass, or any other type of worship environment have other people in the congregation, aside from the clergy, who will minister to them all the time to give them a word of encouragement or confirmation. It's great and all, but at times we take it for granted. I used to as well, until I had someone outside of that norm minister to me about keeping my faith in Christ during my upcoming battles. At the time, I understood him not to believe in Christianity. He was always open and firm about his skepticism on the idea of religion. We spoke about my future career goals, as we were unloading his vehicle. His words were, "If this is what you want to do with your life, you have to keep your love in Christ because you will see the worst that people can offer." I was shocked and somewhat confused. Why would he be talking to me about this? Months later, when I recalled the moment to him and thanked him for the motivation, he didn't even remember saying those words. He remembered what we were doing and talking to me as we were gathering the equipment, but he didn't remember those words! Thank you again, Mr. Frank. Those words are just as true now as they were then.

Even though I moved a lot while growing up, I was never good (and I am still not) at making new acquaintances. I can be extremely introverted with unfamiliar faces. When I started my higher learning, I was far from the people I was used to being around, so there was a lot time for me to listen to The Great Voice. I started what seemed to be a journal at first, but it turned into the threads that are the foundation of this piece. The first insert goes like this.

My Path to God

As I read Augustine's *Confessions*, I found that although it seems there is a good and bad pulling at us, it is merely wills pulling at our soul. To follow The Right Will is to follow "God" and Truth. It is simply a decision to leave carnal desires behind, and though not easy at all, it must be done.

Leaving desires of this world behind is all about breaking habit (natural desires). To break this habit, we must not rely on our strength, but The Strength that is "God". We must, I feel, be ashamed (in the sense of guilt) to do these things. Ask questions. Do I not want to live in heaven with The King? Why is it my soul knows where to turn and how to turn, but it doesn't turn at all?

I've given my life to You, and I do believe my soul is truly saved, but so much has happened since. I have fallen so many times since my baptism in 1995. Even though I've fallen so many times, I give You all my praise, all credit, all adoration and admiration, and all of my trust. But, my Father, is that enough? Do I need to give anything else? I have nothing else. Why do I feel like what I give still isn't my best? But that's all I own, and it's not even mine—it's still Yours, dear Lord.

This was laid on my soul to write, and I have obeyed. May God use this.

You can debate this thread all day, but this was where I was at the time, mentally and spiritually. If you feel like I contradict myself later on, mark it in the growth column because I, like you, have changed, am changing, and surely will change. We should ask ourselves, What are we changing for? Who are we changing into?

Other threads surely followed, and then came the dream that trumped all others. The dream is so pivotal in my life because I have yet to have it all revealed to me. My very existence was also threatened directly, at the end of it. Although I've had moments that suggest I shouldn't be alive, my life wasn't being threatened in the sense of a physical death inside that dream. In fact, it is constantly being threatened on a spiritual level, just like yours. An example of this: What kind of lives are we living if we can't produce? Working limbs and a heartbeat are as useless as a body with no heartbeat if the gifts aren't used to be resourceful to someone or something.

During my junior year of college, shortly after a two-day fast, I was woken out of my sleep, and I heard the word *write*. How did I know I didn't hear *right*? Well, at this time I had already collected so many entries in my tablets and written so many poems that I figured, what else could it have meant? It wasn't until I graduated and made a few career decisions that things fell into place. (A special thank-you to Daniel Ortiz.) This book shall also serve as a testament that when The Higher-Up sends word down for something to be done, you will answer, and it's in your best interest to not be stubborn and do it.

I've given you this quick look into who I am so that we have a better connection. If you've read this far, thank you. But if you're choosing to continue, I wanted you to know why certain words were chosen over others, why the analogies may seem a little off the wall, and why I truly believe He is "the great I AM." I've given you a very brief outline of what I've experienced, but I have given you no detail of what I was feeling and almost no insight to what I was thinking. I've shown you how insecure I still am; however, this work still exists. This is proof that The Automaker will use any vehicle He sees fit to deliver the message. Enjoy!

Near the Roots

Misery

Ms. Erie treads the sidewalks of life's streets
Been with a lot of folks and still invites company.
Claims she has that wet, and you can drown for a fee,
But keep your cash because you can pay her with your peace.
Too many lights on the main, so meet her in the alley,
And you'll get your party there, in the dark of your despair.
And from the driver's chair, you smell the life in her hair
That belonged to all the others; you're her next tally.
The presence of your pity in this party makes her happy;
As she brings her freak out, she's jerking your tears out.
Making the car bounce, but she ain't got exactly
What she wants from Daddy; she'll stay until she kicked or cleans out.
Sexually transmits her sorrows; she gets full and leaves you hollow.
And in your car, you like her there, until you mind is filled with dread,
Locked inside a fogged-up ride, real difficult to leave.
Yes, that ass is phat, but this ain't where you want to be.

Ms. Erie treads the sidewalks of life's streets
Been with a lot of folks and still invites company.
Curves of insanities that are hugged by your fantasies.
You haven't seen her bare, and already you cannot breathe.
She said she relieves, but you feel the pressure
When you undress her and see things you can't believe.
And it's all natural yes, everything is real.
Unfortunately, she can't say the same for herself,

And when you find out what she lied about,
It's hard to pause this game, stop the pain, and pull out.
Your body nears a drought as she's making your tears rain.
You think of how you answered her, when she never called your name.
Sexually transmits her sorrow; she gets full, leaves you hollow.
And in your car, you like her there until your mind is filled with dread,
Locked inside a fogged-up ride, real difficult to leave.
Looking for what's tight, you put yourself into a squeeze.

Ms. Erie treads the sidewalks of life's streets
Been with a lot of folks and still invites company.
She keeps you running from what's real so you can't see yourself,
Because if you ever do, that'll be the moment that you leave.
She suggests you close your eyes as she rides you to your dreams,
Giving you just what you want while taking what you need.
She shows you the pleasures of her dandelion.
Pretty is what you see, but it's not a flower. It's a weed.
But you just want to be right where her rose is,
Forgetting thistles and thorns will make you bleed.
You don't even stop her after she guts you open,
But dozens of roses she gives to those she puts to sleep.
Will death be what it takes?
Why would you wait to open your eyes at your wake?
Temptation is real, but what it yields is fake.
Any promise to a gullible guppy is only bait.

*I*f I'm asked what's bothering me, I usually say obvious things as the next person; maybe it's something financial or relationship issues. But it's deeper than that for all of us. We feel so worn down by the current position because of our preexisting controversy. These are the problems, strife, or demons that we've acquired throughout our earlier years. We claim that time has healed these things, however we've only forgotten about them because of distractions of all sorts. Never settling the conflict will cause self-conflict, and when that is overlooked, it grows and matures with you, in you. Like a woman in labor, you will instinctively give birth to the products of this manifestation any time you feel overwhelmed by daily labor.

Some people are like me, believing that if there were anything negative living off of my hard work and existence, I would have already dealt with it. There is not enough time to run and allow the past to recur. In fact, people with similar mind-sets prefer confronting dissent as it arises. But have you thought that some things can't be truly dreaded if you don't have the necessary understanding? Think about how The Creator hasn't revealed everything to us from the beginning. One reason is because we wouldn't understand most of the information shared until we grasped the concept of its prerequisites. Could you be in bereavement of a loved one if you've never experienced some form of love with him or her? Would sorrow be a factor if you'd never met happiness?

Inflicting harm on a child will certainly hurt them physically. The child may attach the pain to an action and avoid the behavior or situation. Continually harming a child will make that child question why he or she is receiving this undesired attention and what can be done to avoid it. Soon, that child will see that people do similar things to one another when they don't like something about them. With this new understanding, the child may link the harm to not being liked or some other conclusion, depending on his or her daily stimulus. If the child feels that it's because they are not loved, something they believe to be unfair, or something they feel can't be changed, the harm inflicted becomes more agonizing. This is because the physical torment is now being translated to the internal level.

This inner segment isn't harmed or affected physically; however, it is affected by the connections that we make to physical interactions. Those associations or conclusions are products of what we have submerged ourselves in. The phrase "ignorance is bliss" holds some weight on this scale, but know that ignoring any problem entirely means that you're still in it. As we learn in math, we should solve problems in their simplest forms.

Canvases that display viewpoints lacking in hope or self-awareness can make you resentful, create fear that deters you from trusting, or pull your focus away from accepting your faults in a matter. Murals of faith or consciousness can stimulate growth of a mind and a more positive outlook when facing problems. It is a great feat or virtue to push through and excel above your storms, but what are some things that you carry as you carry on? Look at yourself, see whether you may have overpacked for the journey, and unload the accessories you won't need for the trip ahead. Erykah Badu suggests to "pack light," and I agree. The weight of your convictions is enough; don't allow excessiveness to harm you internally in the long haul.

The unnecessary things we pack are shown in the thoughts, words, and actions that we constantly try to justify. We do things to save face or come out on top. We've carried these leeches so long that we nurse them as they siphon good things away from us. When they hunger, you'll take more to satisfy them. At times you reluctantly do these things, but their hunger or pride is projected only in you. You believe this is who you are and that you can't be changed. You always feel short of something because their gluttony is never satiated. Well, it's time to unpack these accessories; they don't match the wardrobe designed for you anyway.

Accomplishing and acquiring are great pleasures, especially when you receive something you desire and have done nothing to earn it. Your own deprivation should be your motivation to seek, not the desire of external factors posing to be your thoughts. You wouldn't take a drink to quench another person's thirst; you wouldn't ask them to eat for you if you're starved. These facts show that to have a fulfilled life is to find the things that you seek, and that to reach for objectives that aren't yours is greed. If these heavy freeloaders did somehow get everything they wanted, what else would you have to gain?

Distinguishing wants from gluttony is as simple as asking, What made you begin the journey, to be hallowed or to be hollow? The former means to be holy, consecrated, or special; the latter can mean to have no significance or importance. Notice that the change of one letter creates two directions of travel. In the same sense, every piece of interference affects your vector. A swivel of one degree from the original destination can throw you miles from the finish if the journey is long enough. With that said, I must say a lot of Christians worship with the interpretation that life after death will be about us. We will be waited on while we live in mansions on streets of gold. But, we're being waited on now. Time is thinning, and the meal is getting cold. Enjoy this life while you have it, but learn that our service is to serve. Eat and be merry.

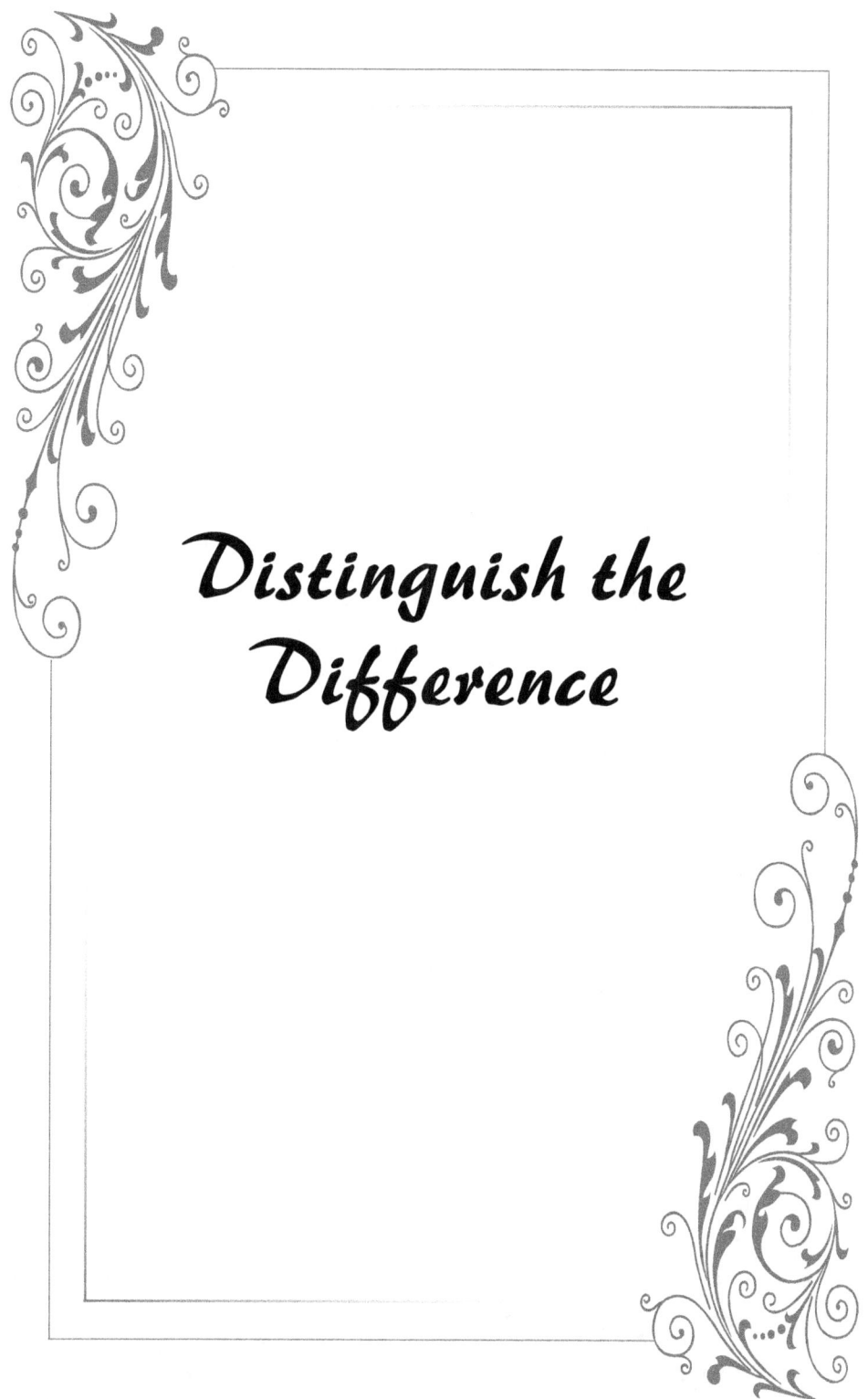

Distinguish the Difference

Tale of Three Warriors

In a far kingdom, there lived three warriors who set out on a quest to achieve a great treasure. Each was known for specific characteristics. One for bravery and strength, one for kind-heartedness and mercy, and the last for good intentions and will. Their names were Ari, the brave; Chesed, the merciful; and Jaasau, the man of action. The champions knew their goal existed, but they did not know where to find it, so they first sought information about the treasure's whereabouts. The warriors were informed they could get their answers from a ruler in a faraway nation, close to where Chesed was born.

When they arrived at that distant land, the warriors found that the kingdom in that land was in the middle of a great war with two neighboring nations. Ari, Chesed, and Jaasau sat together to discuss what to do. Ari and Chesed stated that they would wait until the time was right and then grab the king in the heat of battle, when his guards were worried about the battlefield and not attentive to his position. They agreed on the idea and decided to put it into action. Jaasau thought to himself that this strategy would be so much better if they had to use less manpower. Jaasau figured he could pose as a warrior in one of the other kingdoms and side with the larger force, then there would definitely be no issue in getting close to the king. As Jaasau put his plan in motion, he discovered that the king's army did not have strength in its numbers but in its reasons for fighting. He found himself facing the king's mighty army, and his plan failed. As a result, Chesed and Ari had to pull the injured Jaasau off of the battlefield, nab the king, and get the knowledge they'd journeyed for, all by themselves. This was a dangerous feat for just two warriors.

The king, now in their possession, was very cooperative. He knew of the treasure that they sought, and he told them that so many had failed to even reach it. "More than one mind is needed to see it, but only one mind-set can achieve it," the king told them. Then he pointed them to the north of his kingdom, informing them that the treasure rested inside a glorious mountain that had an altar at its base. Ari and Chesed started the travel northward while also looking after the injured Jaasau.

As time passed and the skies changed, soon Jaasau got better. He was now able to stand and walk on his own. Feeling bad about the situation he'd put Ari and Chesed in, he apologized for his actions and vowed to be a more reliable partner and a bigger help. He proclaimed, "I will be one who will do more for my brothers than they can think of doing for me. I will fight for my fellows like no other!"

As they continued north, Jaasau trained his hardest to make a solid recovery before they reached their destination. Ari advised him to take his recovery slowly, adding that it took time for any injury to fully heal, but Jaasau was determined to stand behind his word. Not far into his training, Jaasau injured himself again, resulting in a fresh wound on his leg. Chesed figured they had traveled far enough to be close to a pond that he heard stories about as a child. He told his friends that this pond was said to heal the injured over a short time. Chesed led them to this pond.

The warriors did not know that the pond was the drinking place for dragons that lived nearby. The three warriors soaked themselves in the waters and laughed at past stories they'd experienced together. Their laughter was cut short when they heard a rustling in the bushes. Not knowing what to expect, Ari and Chesed assisted Jaasau, and they swam to the far end of the pond. When they reached the opposite end, it was apparent to them that they were at the foot of an altar. This altar was placed at the base of a high mountain. "This has to be to the mountain of the treasure," they said. When their conclusion was made, a dragon appeared from the bushes. The three companions decided that the dragon must stay near to prevent travelers from reaching this prize. To avoid any chance of their journey being ruined, they agreed to deal with the dragon now.

Ari and Chesed planned that they should approach from underwater as the dragon drank and make an unexpected attack. They would be able to handle this by themselves, so they told Jaasau to remain where he was and rest. Jaasau felt he was well enough to help and protect his friends. As the other two began their assault on the dragon, he soon followed. Sensing the movement in the water, the dragon stopped drinking and shouted, "I know you're in there! I can feel you move." Chesed and Ari waited for their opportunity. Jaasau was still approaching to help take down the dragon. When Jaasau got close enough, a larger dragon appeared out of the bushes from the same area. The warriors knew they had to abort this plan and devise another strategy. Jaasau could not make the swim back to the far side; he was not fully rested and had used too much breath and energy to get there. He surely could not make the swim back and regroup.

"Why are you shouting?" asked the second and larger dragon. The first dragon answered, "Something is in the water." The larger one studied the water closely and replied, "No, someone is in the water, but I cannot tell how many or where."

Jaasau was running out of air fast and would soon have to give up his position. At the opposite end of the pond, Chesed and Ari knew they had to act fast to save their comrade. They discussed that they each would surprise a dragon from behind as they were focused on Jaasau. Fighting two against two would be a much tougher task for such large foes, but it was still possible. They got out the pond and circled around the treeline. When they arrived at their positions, a third dragon appeared. Their chances were even slimmer, but they still had to save their friend. Jaasau finally rose from the water, and Ari and Chesed soon found themselves fighting for the right to finish their quest toward which they'd patiently worked. It is sad to say that these three warriors were never heard from again.

This story shows how someone's intentions can make one impatient and, in the end, a detriment to self or others around. The goodwill of a person is not always good for the people around him or her, even if one means to help. Waiting for the right time to help others is just as important as wanting to assist them. Patience is an important matter to any action and plan. Stick around and seek the knowledge you want. Work and wait for the recovery you need. Pause and plan for the actions you will take. Don't let your intentions endanger or defile other areas of your character.

These three journeyed on one mission with two separate mindsets. Chesed and Ari wanted to achieve a goal: come to a successful end, carry all the way through, and finish stronger than they'd started. Jaasau wanted to reach a goal and would arrive at it with any form of progression. Jaasau didn't see that there is an order to how things are done. He made mistakes, as we all do. He didn't learn from the danger in which he put his loved ones into. As a result of his decisions, they all suffered. As you heal from wounds of previous fissures and faults, take the time to observe what happened and why things may have crumbled or split in that manner. The frequency of life's tremors may increase if you move too fast. The magnitude of them can't strengthen you if you aren't mindful of how you shift and collide with your surroundings, but what is made from these quakes can be beneficial to you and serve as an embankment to those who will come after you. In the aftermath of a shock ask, What can I see?

Asking what can be seen is a question that should be directed to the self. What new things have I learned from my faults? Is this new understanding optimistic or pessimistic? Can I better the others around me as I better myself with this? These are great answers to seek. Asking what can be seen isn't seeking a handout from another or seeking what can be given to us (like calling for "the blessings from above" that'll help us cut corners). All people want more money for their expenses, but not many people pray for the discipline of spending control. We'd all like our enemies to be dealt with, yet none of us ask for patience and long-suffering so that we can display love to our foes. When you say, "What can I see?" do it with the aspiration to better yourself, not with the mind-set of a fan or groupie. Even though fans and groupies clap, dance for, and scream a name in praise, understand that fans and groupies simply want to see, be entertained, or be quickly pleased by whomever they're currently praising.

The Creator doesn't need us for fame or to verify existence; He wants followers. Followers are loyal. They display devotion by sharing the work of the icon, investing in companies or charities that are attached to their idol. They live day to day with the hope, will, and faith that they will see their hero face to face. You won't catch them wearing apparel only when the star comes to town. They don't move to the next hot trend when it seems their loved star is burning out of gas.

Real followers even know everything about the icon's image, background story, and current issues, as well as their purpose of each creation. Through dedication, followers show themselves approved, not to prove—they don't show their allegiance simply because "that's what's hot in the streets" or "what's popular." Knowing when the next show is, what message the piece of art was aiming to portray, or how the idea for the work came about is a result of the follower diligently seeking to know more about The Artist. This is different from wanting to know that information to fit into a group or reinforce your empty actions. Then all the effort of that following, would be about you—the arrogance of a fan.

Empirical Isn't Imperial

Discovery

They say knowledge is power, and power corrupts.
So did I go to school to learn to self-destruct?
Crack open books, and I can never get enough.
Words flow in constantly, just filling my cup.

I can only take so much before I reach the brim.
Then if I take in anymore, my brain would spill.
That leaves a puddle where somebody can slip.
It being the world's knowledge, there's not much to grip.

Get a foundation, because books can change you.
Reconstruct your heart, making you a stranger.
Frame of the house bent; it's a faulty establishment.
Mind tilted like the tower that sits near Rome.

Tower of Pisa, we can't grab a piece of
Something that is simple. We don't sit; we roam,
Because these false signals have us searching for service.
Or maybe God returned the calls, but we're busy trying to serve us.

An age of denominations, no standing united.
Different doctrines causing war, we sit in church divided.
Got so educated we forgot about The Faith.
Fighting ourselves, seeking knowledge for an arms race.

Someone once told me to try and run on my feet.
That didn't come from a book and not even a page.
No paper involved, not even a sheet,
Though the words have covered, from being enslaved

To false convictions of diction that's purely fiction,
Written by a genius that turns out to be pretentious.
Sure, he thought he was enlightened, and all was in sight.
But his mind was in night, so he was wrong when he did write

Between the lines that rested on upon pages
That then stacked into a ream, to pull us in the dream
That is really a nightmare. But the black horse stops.
Hear the galloping of horses, pulling a chariot of fire.

I had a debate about creation with a close friend of mine who was atheist at the time. It isn't my goal to try to prove people wrong on the matter, but rather to make them question why they hold to their beliefs so tightly. Though he'd read the Bible a number of times, I knew it would be unavailing to use scripture because he didn't believe in it at all. I think he even called it a great story (which it really is, as we're watch things unfold). "It doesn't make sense. Show me facts. Life is based on evidence," he told me. He continued to say, in so many words, that he believed in numbers because numbers were certain. "One plus one will always be two, and two plus two will always be four." There is no need to go into detail about what happened during the debate. This chapter shows what I found in meditation after the discussion. I did tell him that an empirical veil is very thin.

I can only think one man plus one man would be a family of two, and one woman plus one woman would be a family of two, but one man and one woman would soon equal a family of three (and that's not considering twins, triplets, and so on). We're all human, and birth of life shows that one human plus one human will not always equal two humans. This is for anything that reproduces. Life is bigger than numbers. Life is bigger than you and me.

Faith and hope require trust, and trust requires one to be vulnerable. There aren't many people who like feeling defenseless, accessible, or reliant. We find hope in security, we find security in control, and because we can control numbers and things of their likeness, that is where we decide to put our trust. We choose to be susceptible to the tangible experiences of our world or the measurable qualities of existence.

Consider that a lot of what is around us came from the desire to make living easier, yet desire cannot be measured and is not consistent with reality. Take into account that a great deal of technology started with imagination, though imagination cannot be quantified. If there's so much more to us than our five senses, couldn't there be even more to what we call existence? I guess if we knew everything, we could be certain about this concept, but that wouldn't leave any room for faith. If we wanted to know it all, Socrates would advise us to start by acknowledging the evidence that we don't know anything. This is very submissive or vulnerable. So, what will you submit to? At the least, we can construct something that appears to be strong and absolute (economy, governments, social bonds), but faith or hope put in those entities would be just as synthetic as what's made.

I hold confidence in The Creation of life because I know with the bond of a woman, I can create. We could not have taught this to ourselves or learned this by trial and error before succumbing to the forces of nature. I am certain that I carry the seed to the future and that I must render it to the ground so that it can be nurtured, root, and grow. I understand that though the earth can hold her own, the way I till, tend, and reap will affect what she yields in future seasons. I shouldn't litter because I risk the chance of polluting what will be tomorrow. What she and I will create is the tangible substance of what we shared but couldn't measure. Our creation is a direct product of how we worked with one another.

This idea of the circle of life isn't just a cycle stating that everything that begins must end; it is also an analogy or metaphor displaying that if we can create, then we can be created.

Grow, Expand, Improve

The Sword

To be put through the furnace and experience the burning,
Temperature so high you melted to the core.
Never pushed to this degree, once hard, now liquidity,
Just a puddle from the pain and the scorn.

Only to be poured, now fitting a new mold
With a toughening conviction as you grow cold.
Not used to the design, you struggle to keep shape,
Still feeling the flame as you're continually beat straight.

Trying to get balance so that you're easily managed.
Every blow to your will is a test to be wielded,
Inside of battle. This is the reason you're made lighter.
Notice your impurities were burned in the fire.

More intact with you, you'll last longer,
But in the heat of war, that's a sure way to fail.
You made it this far; in the end, you don't want to crumble.
If you want to be steel, more trials will be lived.

Now that you've been made, you seek perfection in your ways
So in the test of time, your strength will not fade.
And to achieve that, just reenter the blaze,
This time to solidify, so you're quickly submerged in ice,

Only to rise even better; now you're dependable.
When the enemy is met, you won't break like you used to,
But stand firm in the contact, reliable in combat.
But come back, we have to sharpen that.

See, a blade is better with an edge.
It must be honed if it wishes to stay ahead.
Cutting through what blocks without a sign of fret,
Separating what's false from what truly Is.

*P*eople can suggest things for you while having your best interests in mind, but if their suggestions are not a part of the plan for your life or coincide with The Planner's itinerary, are their suggestions really for your best interests?

After finishing my degree, I didn't know how I should continue my climb to my end goal. The ones who claimed they would be there for me, if I were to need them, had nothing to offer except "You should…" and "I'll pray for you." We all know advice can be great at times, and prayer is a very powerful thing with works, but at the time I truly needed help. Not a handout, and not pity … just help. I was studying the book of Proverbs around that time, and within a span of three weeks, I had been given the passage Proverbs 3:5 from four different sources. Every time it was seen or heard, the verse stood out. It was the centerpiece to any background, the only words I could remember from the conversations. My Father was screaming to me, "Trust Me despite your position, and lean not on your, the world's, or society's understanding." I didn't get it. Aren't you supposed to listen to your elders and not be hardheaded? The Instructor revealed to me that He can give a whole church the word to move, but if He told you to stay, you'd be better off leaving your vehicle in the parking lot with the emergency brake engaged (just in case).

In my life, I've tried to take heed to the "words of the wise" and avoid major setbacks in life, and it truly works. Listening to your parents will prevent the disappearance of years and hair down the line, but learning new things will challenge you. You'll see contradictions in the morals that you were raised with or previously had. Our parents aren't perfect, and neither were theirs, so how could their morals be?

Seeing new outlooks will question your interpretation of preceding revelations, at times. This happens because stressors and desires create bias. Instead of interpreting things through a clear and precise scope, these stressors and biases create a kaleidoscope, refracting and bending the light of messages in so many other ways, including the originally intended way. The mixing of the unintended with the intended is how confusion is created. Can true growth or development occur if our minds weren't pulled at or stretched in some manner to decipher and clarify things? No, we would simply know more useless things.

I enjoy being comfortable like everyone else. Being encouraged (or what is usually seen as agitated) to grow is uncomfortable to me. It feels a whole lot better to chill out, vibe, and go with the flow. Why must the fight for improvement always be upward and intense? I can simply stay here, where I'm loved and appreciated, where I'm acknowledged and unforgotten, where things are familiar and easygoing. It's from this view that we see it. There's nothing above us trying to retain our progression. There's no real power saying improvement is not an option. The power of growth and self-advancement has already been placed in our hands. Gravity has no effect on this climb. So what is the fight against, if there's nothing vertically keeping us down or oppressed? It's against horizontal comforts.

Horizontal comforts are things and people that are in front of us, as well as the things and people that are currently behind us. We don't want to let go of them. They're the current lifestyles that we don't want to release because of insecurity, fear, or whatever. In fact, they don't have a hold on us—we keep a hold on them. We find a false sense of security or identity in them. We can't grow or change our lives without pulling things out of or changing our lifestyle. Seeing that we are the biggest causes for our stunted growth is choosing to be candid with self. It's not healthy to constantly perceive that someone or something is out to hold us back or oppress us. Every offense given shouldn't be offensive to us. We will never experience real peace and we will never grow where it really matters, if this is our perception. We will never be fit to give advice, help, or lead others.

Being able to give advice geared toward another's best interests is a form of leadership. Leadership gives purpose, motivation, and direction to achieve a goal. Leadership is empty without The Cultivator's growth. Its purpose will be simplified, have vain intentions, lack scope, and present a vague concept. Its motivation is self-centered, making it hard to get others to move in accordance with the plan. The direction will always fall short in communication; the messages of commands or influence will be obscure or elusive to the vision of the next person.

This is why the growth of our lives is important to helping another. Everyone can have the intentions of helping the next person, yet it's what is in us that will determine whether we really are helpful to another.

Two cars that appear to be the same will run differently and have two separate types of emissions from the fuel that is put into them. The car with the most compatible type of fuel, or octane, is environmentally friendly, not leaving a trail of smog as the other would do. Just as we choose our lifestyle, we choose our fuel. The fuel has the same effect on the cars that our lifestyle has on our growth or change. If that fuel affected the lethality of the emissions to the environment, our lifestyle will affect our essence, who we are, and what we give off (e.g., advice). Don't leave a trail of smog behind you; don't eat away at the atmosphere and others' lives frivolously. We should take the time to check our emissions; in fact, to be negligent of our emissions is seen as a fashion of confirmation bias by refusing to pay attention to what we are, just to make others like us. Simply because someone else did it to us.

It's still a personal decision of how much of another's advice we will take into consideration. We shouldn't act on all the consultation we receive because it is still our own roads that we must tread. The aid given may not be for the ailment of our lives. Pass on the input that you don't need. Don't even consider breaking the seal and using a portion of the worthlessness. This usually comes from sources that have never been in your situation or anything relatable to it. These seals can't be mended, and simply putting the lid on or closing the product leaves unfinished or future trouble. Be a good tender of the words you receive; sift through them well. Keep what will help the advancement of your environment.

I'd like you to know that God was willing to spare Sodom and Gomorrah just for the sake of ten righteous ones. I believe The Judge took this into consideration before the sentencing because He knows that change must begin somewhere; it must start on some level. Most of the time, it is on a small level; in fact, in that instance it could have been only ten people. That growth could've started from a unit or group, just as life's evolution begins with an unseen element like the heart or mind. Soon, the things around the element start to change and move around. Layer after layer, the prosperity builds.

Take the world around you for an example. It is all a result of what happened moments before, like a graduation of what was here earlier. This picture also shows that it's important to be attentive to the schools that we attend, meaning the suggestions for which we look to others.

The advocacy you seek and discover from others will change as you do. That's normal because your understanding is improving, and the things you want to know will have more substance and sustenance suitable for your life. That type of understanding and knowledge is claimed by a lot, touched by some, but truly held and shared through an even smaller group. It all starts with self. That piece of you that you always wanted to get rid of or remodel, but you thought it was always insignificant while saying, "I'll get to it later." Growth starts on the smallest level, no matter how unnoticed the initial reaction may be.

Perception

The Best View

Being where I'm from, seeing what I've seen,
I feel more death has been caused by clichés.
Locked in traditions for many generations,
Half the things we do is just because of genetics,
Been engrained within our DNA.
See the destruction of the past, but refuse to make another way,
All because Mama and Daddy did it.
Want the benefits of a relationship that you're not truly real with.
Never fully submit; figure knowing who He is, is enough.
Still thinking your faith is going to shake the world up,
Feeling it's your duty to reach and save a soul.
Like it's guaranteed the right path is the one that you're on,
Or clean hearts are scrubbed by the beliefs that you own,
When yours is not as clean as The Star of the dawn,
As if salvation repels sin with a bubble.
But filth disguised as faith is just religion.

Just want you to see the make of your ambition
Because desires of the heart can be influenced by the eyes.
Processing with your feelings instead of with your mind,
Following plans that they made when they could've drawn them blind.
Maybe they were seeking eternal life.
But a prize so great can gift internal lies,
Not to just be invited to the winner's circle.
Because like the flesh, the soul doesn't want to die.

A fire fed by the scripts, you know.
Ironic how we learn to get more irrational,
Trying to claim healing water to douse flames
When removing oxygen would do the same.
So keep your mind higher, don't fight the suck of the vacuum.
When you are in space, that's when you find you
Mystery solved, no more a missing child.
So we'll toss the milk carton, to seek solid food.

I often think about The Truth. Where am I in relation to It? I search and I seek, but so many other minds have come before me. Who knows how much of the truth has been compromised, and why? We tend to change or pervert the truth as it is passed from one person to the next. Emotions, past encounters, and what we mentally digest are all reasons for this. Lost information in translations and paraphrasing almost make this seem like a very extensive game of telephone. As the truth is given to another, what is perceived and inferred doesn't always concur with what is being projected and displayed. Perception is such a tricky matter. We must be cognizant of our mind-state when we're receiving knowledge from and giving knowledge to outward sources.

Perception is what will affect interaction and resiliency. Going through hard times can be seen as a test of improvement, or it can be envisioned as a setback. Having a negative perception can make you antagonistic or deter you from seeking happiness. Strife will always be adversarial in your eyes. Opposition and disagreement won't be used to better you, if you lived with a bleak outlook. You'd carry a chip on your shoulder or have a depressed mind-state. You'd be weak and weary from being woe. We can't always be above, successful, or esteemed at all times. Can you imagine a person that had the heart and mind to dream, the vision and wit to know how to find the start to this journey, and the will and motivation to go and get that success—but the person lacked the strength to grasp it or the determination to hold on to it? To have all that labor completed, but be too weak to harvest—what was the point of the dream? Hard times are needed in life; they build endurance and patience, if we allow them to. Why would you want to be exalted above the rest, only to drop the ball at some point? You'll find more shame failing with the crowd looking at you than you would find failing among the crowd.

Having a positive perception about adversity can promote humility and gratitude. If you can be happy in gloomy times, you can surely have joy in the good times. That surplus of joy will be greatly appreciated by those around you. If you can fight in the presence of slim odds, then you will have no problem battling when the odds are in your favor. The extra strength will be great service to others. Have joy in your suffering because just like your blessings, it is given. It is all allowed by Permission. No king has ever risen on his own strength and effort. All glory gained is glory given, and your perception will determine how you'll reign and how you'll fall.

Perception will cause an overlap as we share with others. Things like honesty and truth will coincide in our minds, in the times where a connection between them doesn't exist. Honesty is being open; it is what is true about your situation. It is a record of your account, your point of view. A lot of the time, honesty is just your opinion. Truth is factual. It can stand on Its own, and there's no need of evidence or justification. This distinction means that just because something is spoken from the depths of our hearts, minds, and souls, the words aren't automatically validated in Truth, no matter how wise they may seem. I've come to believe that wisdom is based in Truth if it can be used at all times, no matter what subject. This shows that we all lie at times, even the ones that always "I tell it how it is" and "I keep it real". The fact of the matter is bluntness and sincerity have nothing to do with validity. Truth is Itself.

We shouldn't be found in our own realities at all times, choosing to remain ignorant of what and who is around us. Ignorance begets complacency. Complacency develops in adolescence and matures into tradition, rituals, and then religion. It ultimately meets its death at the age of staleness, preventing change. Ignorance can lead to fear, and fear can lead to more shortcomings. We should constantly seek The Truth, being willing to disprove our own theories and change our personal laws. This is a mind-state of growth.

I had a combat-lifesaver instructor say, "Soldiers want to be trained. They just don't know it." He repeated this every lesson for a whole week. It made sense to me simply because we don't always know what we want, and we spend a lot of time avoiding the situations that can give us that answer. Then I thought, *How many people want to give their lives to Jesus Christ and don't know it?* So many other things, that won't matter when we die, may grab our attention. Maybe we feel a lack of Hope but can't explain it, even though we have what others call success. But success shines as different colors in the eyes of man than it does in the eyes of Reality, and so does failure. That thought led to, *How many people think that they are okay with Jesus Christ just because they are nice and well-mannered individuals?* These are just some thoughts, however it's a supervisor's duty to initiate the growth of the soldier. This means that it's a leader's purpose to promote growth in others. You can't properly do this while being stuck in your own little reality.

I also understand a lot of people agree that perception is only their standpoint, and that it is not always the truth. They are in tune with themselves and are aware of their surroundings, but they still don't believe in anything beyond this universe. Truth is what can be proven to them. Therefore, I draw a scenario. We have a red ball. We throw the ball in a shed that we also throw everything else in, and we forget about the ball. In time, we need a ball. We are very positive that we have one. The shed shuts out all light, and it is filled with shelves, buckets, and other random things. We invite a skeptical friend of ours to help look for the ball in the dark. This shed represents our perception. We will only know what we touch, and we will only be able to describe to one another what we feel and believe. We find impatience and a few bumps on our heads before we ever find the ball. You and I are sure that the ball is in the shed, but our friend isn't too sure about our claim. Though our friend knows that it is possible for the ball to be in, beside, over, or under something, it is also possible for us to be wrong. Maybe we misplaced it, got rid of it and forgot that we did. Maybe you and I are simply imagining just because we want to believe in something that will give us hope or joy. There are so many other things that suggest the ball isn't in the shed to our friend.

The majority of doubt is based in our human error. In this situation, we were forgetful. But in life, we can be overzealous, timid, or flat-out wrong in our understanding. These errors make spreading The Truth a difficult feat. The remaining doubt is based in what we don't consider. In the example, the properties of the ball, the amount of effort that was put into throwing the ball into the shed, the manner that it was thrown in, and what was previously in the shed will collectively have an effect on where the ball went.

An example of something we don't consider in life could be why Adam hid himself. Was Adam ashamed to show God his sin, or was he afraid to show himself? Are we Christians shamed to say that we've previously failed our Father, or are we afraid to say we've been wrong at times as a community? Oh well! The point is we won't change our friend's perception in the matter until one of us finds the ball—The Truth.

The shape of this planet shows us that up and down correlates to one's current position. My down will vary from another person's down when that person is standing on the other side of the world. That is the essence of perception, but with all that distance between us, what is real doesn't vary. Just as there can be a difference in directions depending on your location, there are many deviations of the truth due to perception. The Truth Itself will not change. Just as the Earth's core will be what you point down to, The Truth will always be at the center of what we currently know. The vast existence we call space will always be up because we are engulfed in it, and The Truth will be above and extend beyond any lie. Again, we are physically shown that there is only one Absolute, and there is no other way of coming to know It without having an open heart and mind to what surrounds us. Don't say, "Perception is reality." Let's say that, "perception is reality until we know The Truth." If you continue believing anything else after that, you're just being difficult.

The Plan

Don't Forget Me

It's a killer. I'm talking impatience.
Would've showed you everything if you had waited,
But you served your desire, and your eyes grew
Large enough to see you, and so you ate it.

I would've fed you all the knowledge that you needed.
You felt that was too long of a process.
See, you want it your way because you are conceited,
More satisfied with fast food, even that's processed.

Less wait for that preparation.
Makes you feel like you're full, but it lacks sustenance.
Like hours upon hours, you fill your head with books,
But when it comes to wisdom, you lack substance.

And that's something that I'm full of.
Finding acceptance outside of Me is fool's love.
I know that's too big for your eyes to see,
But as your problems dilate, know you won't forget Me.

I have thoughts of doubt appear in my mind, yet I still believe. Why? One reason is the amount of mercy that is shown in text that I read. Genesis 2:16–17 shows me that the biggest fault that Man could've committed in that disposition was the indulgence of the tree of the knowledge of good and evil. Verses later, we see Man committing that act. In my mind I say, *You were specifically told to not do ONE thing! And you still didn't walk away from that situation? Then when confronted about your wrongdoing, with a mind of "a god", you indirectly blame it on your Creator? Not a good idea, Jack.* But instead of erasing what was present, The Curator saw fit to restore. Then I realize that the plan physically put into action then is the exact illustration of the spiritual plan functioning for my life when I commit that ONE fault and blame everyone and everything else for my fall.

I know of the cheaters in this religion. I see how a church contributes to banks; in return, those banks mistreat citizens by not sharing those benefits. It's nothing other than a bed of lies covered in sheets of hope. But aren't swindlers everywhere? I am aware of the radicalism and nationalism that exists in the religion of my belief. It has caused and is causing wars, dehumanization, and unnecessary death. You will always have those who are overzealous, and others will be without zeal; in fact, every spectrum has two ends of extreme.

Don't allow the choices of someone else to determine what you will believe in because soon you will lose sight of your direction. The Constructor has made a path specific to you. No one will benefit from it but you. Three- and twelve-step plans won't work for everybody. Again, an entire church can be told to pick up and move, but if one member is instructed to stay, it would benefit that person to not move.

Be firm in your instruction; believe you're important enough to be spoken to by The Almighty. Trust what you receive.

I feel that a real ruler has no need of tricking those in the domain to make them heed. I don't think you'll run across devout believers in Christ who will say they were tricked or forced into believing. I say this knowing that things in the Christian faith have been lost and tampered with in the past, but I also say it knowing that real devotion will uncover what is lost and sort what has been tampered with. Just as real devotion has shown me that "god" is a word used to label mystic beings in Greek culture, it has revealed to me that Who I believe in is my All.

Our relationship with Christ is compared to a marriage because of the amount of love that is required to be married to someone that isn't you. Accepting your faults will always be easier than accepting another's faults. Things would be simple if we only had to worry about the talents, skills, and potential of athletes, however we have to welcome their penalties, turnovers, and injuries as well. Taking the beneficent with the maleficent is only possible in love; in fact, love is done, not just felt. I draw the analogy of a franchise because an entire game plan is drawn to get the most productive results out of each player, but each player must sell out to the plan and, most importantly, the team. There will be frustration with lost matchups, battles, and games, yet each season may still be won with patience. Every dynasty that achieved the hall of fame accomplished the feat by rising above the failures inside and outside the lines, to conquer the next challenge.

Mercy, and many other things, is given to me unconditionally. I haven't done anything to even earn this favor. This differs from what an oppressor does. An oppressor gives what the subjects see as delicacies. These finer things are given in control to make the value of them seem higher. These treats are given in hopes of keeping revolt at bay, and if revolt should manifest, the lack of having these delicacies during the stages of rebuilding will make the free desire to be subjected again in some way. In actuality, that oppressor doesn't give anything of real value; in fact, that oppressor keeps the objects of real value (what the subjected needs) to himself. Giving subjects real valued objects whenever they desired them would imply that they are free and equal. We see this truth with the Israelites during their wandering in the desert; some wanted to return to Egypt for meat and other things. The Israelites didn't need meat in the desert because they had endless manna, but the taste of meat would've been convenient and nice to have. The truth shows in the rise of sharecropping after the American Civil War; freedmen worked for rent of land instead of pioneering new land. Sharecroppers went back to what they knew because of their circumstances and having nowhere to go, which suggested that going back would be the easier path. A compromise with your previous oppressor doesn't make you free. This truth is relevant as we search for meaning in life. We struggle to let go of the idea of "I" (the oppressor) being first. Admitting that there is Something greater than what we know or see would be saying that the current power "I" (your oppressor) has given is nothing. Conceding to The Truth that this is all created is saying our opinions really don't matter most of the time, that we don't have any control outside of our perception, and that all of our wants and so-called needs are second in the whole scheme of things. The lack of power that your oppressor has given you shows that the oppressor has no power to give. You must bind yourself in Freedom to be free of bondage.

I think of how a rock cannot withstand running water. It is eventually broken into pieces, and those pieces will be broken down into sand, at some point in time. Sand, however, withstands flowing water by allowing itself to be carried by the water. Rock in its smallest state withstands running water better. You must decrease yourself to gain Real Power.

At times I can't help but feel that I'm in the best possible spiritual situation. Anytime I think about my spiritual position, my mind and heart are at ease; in fact, my core and my essences feel as if I can't be disturbed. I want to share everything that I've seen, though I know I haven't seen it all.

It's like finding that great deal at a store to which you've never been. The deal was so good that you tell the story of your whole day to make your find sound that much sweeter. You've bought what you wanted and are reaping the benefits of having it. You want others to enjoy it as well. Well, have you ever thought how much the seller has benefitted? The seller can look forward to more business from you and can also expect the hearers of your story to make a visit at some time. You've received credit for looking good or making the item's taste desirable, and the seller received credit from you for making the item acquirable. I believe this is what The Seller sought in giving us Jesus Christ: a Gift so great at a price so affordable. You can keep the pleasure and credit that the world will give you, however be sure to say where you got The Find from. The Seller will make the sell.

You and I

Like Me

From the ground, flesh was formed; from the flesh, we are born.
So that means physically we will never be torn from this earth.
Made right from the dirt,
So carnally we're everything that it's worth.
Thoughtfully the same regardless of how you mind works.
Doesn't matter if you believe the egg came first.
Ideas still come from the same yolk,
And that same yolk still has the same growth.
We all think the same: the proof is here for show.
Our boats float the same, though there are different strokes.
Still the same song, though we sing different notes,
And we take different paths traveled with the same hope.
Difference of me and you is the past and points of view.
Because we stand on different planes, we may believe in different things.
But our brains work the same, a trademark from the place where we came,
Shipped out and altered from the things that we've seen.

Say that you dread this world; no one can be trusted.
That means you've forsaken yourself; I ask when was it.
Advocates and enemies can both bind your feet.
You can drown in blood and water, but both are necessities.
Think that you're guarded with a shield, when contact is really shied.
Say your walls are just force fields; you're using them to hide.
A heart doesn't leave because it's not seen,
But wounds will heal, and you can always sew a sleeve.

So I say flaunt it proudly,
Regardless of the things that are sure to scratch it.
Yeah, they'll try to jack it, but don't fret the thieves.
Something they can't achieve if they don't take the whole jacket.
Work to keep loving, let your hands become callused.
And keep your balance, not letting pain's challenge evoke.
Feelings that manifest into actions, then tainting your soul.
Before the movement of your soles, remember love's unconditional.

Regardless of the past encountered, don't keep covered;
Then there is no opening to be filled.
Even a thin filter corrupts a genuine lover.
Nutrients of a gift would be sifted by the film.
Malnutrition will cause a stunted growth.
And the strength of the relationship you'll never know
Not to mention the state of your existence.
The imbalance of your contents will affect your scope.
Lack of trust in others stems from distrust in self.
Worry of stolen riches will take focus from wealth.
The love that is handed down to successors.
They'd be indebted to hatred due to grudges of the ancestor.
I aim to change the connotation of enemy,
So they and thee have no animosity.
Not against one another, but against the problems seen,
So that today's future can start tomorrow's dream.

*W*e are here for a purpose. We were made resourceful on purpose so we can help and love those around us. We can't make others accept our extension of favor; we can control only the amount of sincerity in which it is given. If others refuse your help, leave the gift there and continue on the journey. We must continue to allow ourselves to be used. We can't be hurt by rejection or misuse. Find other ways to be of assistance, but don't hold grudges because you were taken for granted or denied. Remember that we all misuse and take for granted the talents and gifts that have been given to us.

Be as understanding as Empathy is with us. Empathy doesn't agree with everything that we do, but Empathy understands our situations and how they affect us as individuals. A closed mind will not allow us to understand the next person. A closed mind will create prejudice and build boxes in which to place not only others but ourselves as well. The ego will tell us that prejudice is okay, that we're right because "I am different". But our differences are different alike. An ego is as full as what is filling it. All of the filling and feeling of the ego will fade with us. What was done and experienced with it will be forgotten. Therefore, what is left is what was always an empty ego.

It's okay to realize the potential that rests inside of us, but we must also recognize the potential that lies in others. Remember that we're all resourceful on purpose. Acknowledging another doesn't make us less of who we essentially are. To fear doesn't always mean to be afraid; in fact, to consider, to hold regard, and to hold honor of another are also meanings of the word *fear*.

Accept the fact that we don't have it all or know it all. Being human means that I can't put the faults of the next person past myself. Given the right amount of circumstances in the right order, any one of us is capable to falling where our neighbor does. If people decide to put their faith in humankind's knowledge (that we will soon know all, that we'll live as long as we can survive, and that there is no Higher Power), I can't be negative or spiteful toward them and their belief. If I too believe in the schools, sciences, and numbers so far known to this world, then I am capable of putting my faith in humankind's knowledge and wisdom as well. I must understand others' beliefs.

I've gone to this view because I hear a lot of my fellow Christians say in spiritual debates, "Believe half of what you see and none of what you hear." How would any of us be Christians in the first place if we all did that? Think about all of the phenomena you've personally witnessed and believe half of it. Now think of the prophecies that have come to pass from the Bible and the phenomena told to you by prophets in the Bible, others, and books. Now believe none of that. Why would you ever believe in Jesus Christ and the Promise now? I know—it's ironic.

We have to learn to love differently, in a manner that will allow us to understand the differences we have among ourselves. This Love screams humility instead of conceitedness: "I want because I need," not "I need because I want." This Love will cause us to continue through our plight. Instead of giving up on one another after experiencing that bitter taste of failure or hurt, we'll see that the sensation thereof simply means that we are still alive to lend and love more. This Love shows us the wrong that we witness in life may also serve as a clue of what right does not consist of.

I can't allow my experienced pain to cut me short of my usefulness. I understand that despite your view of who or what I am, I have something for you, and you have something for me. If I dismiss you because of discrimination, I dismiss myself in some form. We can make one another better.

The Willie Lynch Letter is a creative (and fictitious) writing sample that was printed in the late 20th century. The writing attempted to paint the mentality of American slave owners, by having a successful slave owner give a speech on "the secret" of how to effectively maintain power on a plantation. It spoke on how to break individuals and make them subjects, as well as how to destroy a people in a way that they will work and not revolt, making them live on your terms and perpetuating their bondage. It aimed at taking away things that make any group a people. Things like culture, generational bonds, and communion among gender are important to any civilization. Taking these pieces will make them reliant on their position and promote agony among them. It spoke in terms of strategy so that you don't have to physically harm or take things to kill a people or nation. It spoke about creating factions and how to make those factions think that they're better than the next in some way. The idea took focus off of the real reason of one's bondage and put that attention toward things that pale in comparison to the real problem.

It has happened in nearly every colony that has been created. A foreign people move in and assume control and take what they came for while creating friction between the native people. Then when the resource is gone or no longer needed, the foreign power evacuates and leaves behind all of the created confusion. Soon those who were once colonized will be at war with themselves, and the warring will last as long as the hate, confusion, and denial ensues.

It doesn't happen only with countries trying to be world powers—it's being done to us, and it's happening within us. It's suggested that you give enough of what's good and give abundantly of what's not needed so that trust among neighbors, pride in the community, and dignity within oneself can be taken without notice. The Lynch Letter placed the bet on the deprived people to take pride in what is given, and they would then believe that their destruction was nonexistent if they felt safer and more superior than before. The people would feel that they were on the rise if they had something better than the next group or class. They would believe that their fall could not be caused by their own hands but by something that truly didn't matter, if they had someone different to blame. "How could I be destroyed if I see no battle being physically fought? I have what I was told I needed, so how am I lacking? It's not my fault; it's because of someone or something else."

The Willie Lynch Letter inferred that if these phenomena could take place within a person and ultimately in a group of people, one could eradicate or subjugate a people without the effort that was being used in the earlier stages of the slave era. This strategy isn't withheld to the idea of slavery; it can be used to destroy anyone anywhere and at any time. What the Lynch Letter depicted is true for any color of people and every civilization that existed. This ideology can be used to harm others, but that doesn't negate its factualness. This deception is like any other and is simply a distraction. The Truth is always present.

Focal Point

This We Will Defend

Why keep it, try to protect it,
When it's the reason for all of this distance?
Why love it, give it affection,
If it's the cause of all misdirection?

As it manifests, we do our best
To make it grow and stretch,
But when it blows our minds,
That is when we call it stress.

Cultivate until it breaks,
And we're at wit's end.
Things that will attack us
Are the things that we'll defend.

If you've decided to stick with me this far, I hope you've understood the latent message, but just in case you haven't, I'll make it clear. Our problems don't begin with religion, global warming, or even guns. Our current issues begin with us. We are the problem. I don't mean our existence; however, what we allow to exist within us is the problem. I'm not aiming to be negative. I simply want to bring attention to fact.

Ever notice there's always a hole in the storyline or a scene of a movie, or that there is always a glitch or technical problem in the virtual worlds that are created? We constantly create imperfection. This place would be worse than what it is, and there would be no chance of making a situation better, if we were truly the last judgment in this creation. There's not one thing physically around us that stands entirely on its own without starting from somewhere and existing without affecting something else. That's why I believe that this Life, and the cycle of It, is perfect—and that we pervert it. Because of that, I know that it's impossible for one person or group of people to control things entirely, regardless of how strategic a system may be.

My parents taught me that there's a difference in what people can do and what they are willing to do. People can see and call you great, yet they may not want you to be great. No one can deny you anything that is meant for your life. We must stay vigil in resilience. To be resilient, we must first be patient. It's okay to cry about our hardships, but not on the battlefield. If we should be hurt or ashamed, we don't have to hide because of it; in fact, our weaknesses can make us strong. Resilience is not having pride. Pride is how the weak run and hide in their fear of being hurt and shamed. Being resilient will allow a wound to scar, and scar tissue is far tougher than what was originally there. Don't allow failure to be the unnoticed roommate, or time will seem like it has blown right by. When you wonder, *How did these years pass me by?* the only answer will be, "Day by day." You must take these opportunities as they come, one at a time. You all won't see Ezekiel's vision of a wheel in a wheel, but all people may choose to see the will of the Will.

Rise every day with the intention of giving your best efforts to yourself and the people with whom you will come in contact. We can't allow the imperfections of our lives to be excuses of poor effort. Moreover, make it easier for others to accept you, and for you to accept yourself. Excellence should not only be sought after; we must discern it just as much as we strive for it. We can be a detriment to ourselves if we don't define what being great is.

It's natural that we will complicate things in our lives, even though life was made simple for us. I see that things were made simple for us in the scene of the Pharisees asking Jesus, "What is the first or most important commandment?" Jesus stated it was to love the Lord your God with all your heart, soul, and mind. In His reply, he also says to love your neighbor as you love yourself. Notice the first part to His answer involves the first five commandments Moses brought down the mountain, in Deuteronomy. Anything that we love with all of our essence will be first. It won't be replaced by something else with a false value. We would set a specific time for it. It wouldn't be involved in our vanity. We would uphold other principles that coincide with it. The second part to Jesus's answer incorporates the second five commandments Moses gave that day. If we loved others with the patience that we love ourselves with, we wouldn't murder anyone. We wouldn't steal from them. We wouldn't cheat them, cheat on them, spread rumors about them, or step on them to achieve our goals.

The answer given by Jesus makes things a little easier for us now. There's no strain to remember the specifics of the Ten Commandments spoken by Moses on that day. I even believe that the ten Moses chiseled into those tablets that day was given to make things simple for the chosen nation at that time. I'm trying to point out the fact that things are continuously made simple for us—we make them more complex while also setting snares for ourselves.

No fire burns without a source of oxygen, fuel, and heat. With every breath we take, we can provide the oxygen to our flames. Issues as we view them couldn't exist without human involvement in some shape or form. Would the problems in your personal life be existent without you being alive? It's because we are a link in the cycle of things; in fact, we're a fundamental link from a Christian's standpoint of view. I once told an old friend who tried to escape an unhappy situation that if she didn't realize the role that she played in a predicament, it would recur in some fashion no matter how far she moved away from the current one. I told her that a clock may not have voice in the environment to where it hangs, but even a broken clock has a say in what it will display. You decide whether to display the right thing only two times per day or to do the right thing the whole day.

We will make our decisions based off of the fuel that we have. The fuel to any problem is the knowledge that we have. There's no such thing as the existence of good or evil knowledge, there is only the existence of the knowledge of those traits. By this, I mean being raised in the Church, being sheltered from the world and its influences all of your life, and only learning who and what God is to the world will not make your thoughts or decisions good by default. If that knowledge was just good, then the fruit of it would be good. But because it's knowledge of what's good, it's totally up to you what will be made of it. Fallen angels have more knowledge than we do regarding who God is, yet they've still fallen. If knowledge was simply good or evil, the All-Knowing wouldn't be as consistent in His ways as we claim Him to be. In knowing all, He knows evil. The one we call Satan wouldn't be as bad as we believe, because he knows good as well. We decide whether or not that knowledge will be applied—and moreover, we decide how it will be applied. You are hereby responsible for all of your actions.

The application of our fuel is usually based in our emotions or heat. We have the choice to make our decisions in a close-minded (quick and rash manner) or in an open-minded (steady and reserved manner). It is up to us to step out of our current emotions and make decisions. As a Christian, I do believe that we were all made in the image of The Original. All of the emotions that we feel, from love to wrath, are emotions that aren't foreign to The Creator of them. There are many examples in the Bible of wrath being withheld during chastisement. If we were handled in the amount of frustration that we cause, things would be grimmer today. I believe one difference in us and Him is that we don't know how to detach ourselves from that emotion to make the best choices in every situation. Simply because we were made in a specific manner, doesn't mean we operate in that manner.

Continually focus on getting rid of the negative growth that lives within every one of us. It has spent years developing inside, so it's going to take more time to defeat it and ultimately separate from it. Fight to get and keep the control of your life and energy.

Recycle

It Won't Stop Until

It won't stop until …
I'm able to communicate on another's level.
It won't stop until …
I acknowledge that atheists may not believe, but their hearts beat. That their minds think, and those thoughts grieve, and that grief stems from the same fears that are within me.
It won't stop until …
Black history is a part of our history, Mexico is also seen as North America, and we understand that capitalism can be viewed as terrorism.
It won't stop until we add brown, red, and yellow in the war on racism.
It won't stop until …
I see myself in my neighbors and realize the weight of their malfeasances is no greater.
It won't stop until …
It won't stop …
But for those who want it to, love those who don't love you.
Because the truth is it can stop.

*M*aybe I take things too seriously. You may feel I have a hard time enjoying myself. It's possible that this is my excuse for being detached at times; you may think that I'm pessimistic. I probably have fewer friends because no one wants to be around a buzzkill. But maybe there's a chance that I'm right on the money with all of this. The fact of the matter is acknowledgment doesn't create Existence, and the lack of acknowledgment doesn't debunk Existence.

I want to be another confirmation for our eyes and say that there is a connection of one life to another. From person to person, there will always be a likeness, whether it be tangible or intangible. There's also a bridge from our race, the human race, to other species. Maybe the connection is in body structure, like opposable thumbs or the count of chromosomes on the biological plane, or maybe the bridge is the amount of compassion or territorial nature we and the other species show to our children or others in our groups or herds. If all of this came from a single Source, shouldn't there be resemblances throughout creation? Simply how siblings are to a set of parents.

Don't be so caught up with the idea of believing or not believing right now. Be informed of the beliefs and schools of thoughts that came before you. We all have to start from somewhere. All of us have to get further away from The Beginning to get closer to The End. If we cut ourselves off from this Growth, we'll become stagnant. We would simply be treading water, far from The Start and The Finish. That's when storms start to seem longer, more tedious, and more troublesome.

Knowing what came before is the only way real progress can be prepped. Without knowing the start of how we think and why we react the way we do to our situations, any circle or lateral movement will seem like real increase. With this fact, would you still say that I take things too seriously?

We were given preinstalled course correction. It's a part of who we are and what we desire. Always wanting things to be better for ourselves and the ones whom we are close to is an example of this course correction. We should allow this programming to run its software in our everyday lives. It's done by showing all of "me" to the next person. If you want this autocorrect to work, never hide who you are (your mistakes). Yes, control how and when you present yourself, but don't contain or lock it away. When the truth of self, which is honesty, is revealed, our questions will be answered. What direction should we take in life? Who should be in our lives, and for how long? What should we believe in? These are pieces we already have to this puzzle. Honesty forces us to search ourselves, and we all know things are found when we search. So search yourself, your temple. Something may be found in your pockets or under one of the many rugs of distractions. Now, with this hope that is shown, would you still believe me to be a pessimist?

I can't stress it enough: accept who you are. Be real about what is going on in your mind and your heart to allow yourself to go higher. Remember that everyone won't accept you, and you won't accept everyone else. But we can all try to understand our neighbors. Great minds have told us that civilization is measured in how well we can disagree.

Because you can be honest about who you are and where you're at, you will be further along in this journey than others. That means an open mind and heart are even more important to effectively communicate with those who don't understand themselves that well. They seek an answer or hint to an answer in you and in your honesty with yourself. In the preface I asked, What do you allow to control you? What things will you allow to control that fraction of you? The things that we allow to fill us and be in our presence will have an effect on what is displayed to those with whom we share. We are all vessels. Regardless of the vessel, the contents are what will be served. Put in the things that will be fruitful. Do you feel that sense of responsibility, in that part of you that people can't see with their eyes? That's The Proof that I spoke of before.

Now, knowing we must be mindful of our entertainment and indulgences, am I still just being a buzzkill? I would understand if you felt that I am, but I believe that you have thought about these things before. I simply want to point out that acknowledging this light will aid you in seeing a better life.

www.ingramcontent.com/pod-product-compliance
Lightning Source LLC
Chambersburg PA
CBHW071422070526
44578CB00003B/661